Evidence of Red: Poems and Prose

LeAnne Howe, an enrolled citizen of the Choctaw Nation of Oklahoma, is an author, playwright, filmmaker and scholar. Born and educated in Oklahoma, she's lectured in Japan, Jordan, Romania, and Spain. *Shell Shaker*, Howe's first novel, received an American Book Award in 2002 from the Before Columbus Foundation. In 2003, she was named Wordcraft Circle Writer of the Year, 2002, Creative Prose. *Equinoxes Rouge*, the French translation for *Shell Shaker* is the 2004 finalist for Prix Medici Estranger, one of France's top literary awards. Currently she is assistant professor in the Department of American Indian Studies at the University of Minnesota. In September 2005, she will be an associate professor in the Departments of English, and American Indian Studies at the University of Illinois, Urbana-Champaign.

Earthworks Series
Series Editor: Janet McAdams

Evidence of Red

POEMS AND PROSE

LEANNE HOWE

SALT

CAMBRIDGE

PUBLISHED BY SALT PUBLISHING
PO Box 937, Great Wilbraham, Cambridge PDO CB1 5JX United Kingdom

© Leanne Howe, 2005

The right of Leanne Howe to be identified as the
author of this work has been asserted by her in accordance
with Section 77 of the Copyright, Designs and Patents Act 1988.

First published 2005

Printed and bound in the United Kingdom by Lightning Source

Typeset in Swift 9.5 / 13

ISBN 1 84471 062 9 paperback

SP

1 3 5 7 9 8 6 4 2

For DR.

Contents

Acknowledgments

The Past:
To the Choctaw Code Talkers of WWI who fought in the Meuse-Argonne campaign in which 171 Germans were captured by Joseph Oklahombi.

To the Choctaw Code Talkers of WWII (including my late uncle Schlicht Billy) who used Choctaw to relay messages in campaigns from Africa, Sicily, Italy, and Germany.

The Present:
To Paula Anderson, Maureen Aiken, Alberta Blackburn, Andrea Carlson, Claire Cardwell, Brenda Child, Carol Cornsilk, Mary Deshazer, Jill Doerfler, Jane Hafen, Patrice Hollrah, Carol Miller, Jean O'Brien, Tricia Plouseh, Michelle Raheja, Heidi Stark, and Emily Wilson, for keeping the sisterhood alive.

To Susan Power, my true sister. For all her support, always.

To poets and writers Jennifer Kidney, Ken McCullough, Robert Tisdale, Robert Trammell, and Michael Seward.

To Geoff Cohen, John Ganim, George Haggerty for that warm March day in Riverside California when the talk turned to cannibals and other lovers.

The Future:
To Jim Fortier for capturing the images. And all the ones to come.
To J.F. Wilson and Ana Mendieta with love.

To José Alvarez López, Joseba Arregi, and Urtzi Arriaga for introducing me to pintxos.

To Kim Meyer for teaching me the value of modern trickster rabbits.

To Harvey Markowitz and Craig Howe for seeing red in the land.

For Janet McAdams and Chris Hamilton-Emery for their belief in my work, and for bringing it to the page. I would also like to thank the editors of the various journals and anthologies in which some of these stories and poems were published:

"Indians Never Say Good-bye" in, *Reinventing the Enemy's Language*, W.W. Norton. New York.

"The Red Wars" in *American Indian Literature*, Revised Edition, University of Oklahoma Press. Norman.

"Choctalking On Other Realities" in *Sister Nations: Native American Women Writers on Community*, Minnesota Historical Society Press. St. Paul.

Grinnell Magazine, Vol. 31, # 2. Grinnell.

Cimarron Review, #121, Oklahoma State University. Stillwater.

"The Chaos Of Angels" in *Callaloo*, Vol. 17, #1. Johns Hopkins University Press. Baltimore.

"Evidence Of Red" in *Nebraska English Journal*, Vol. #38.2. Lincoln.

"Hashi Mi Mali" in *Gatherings, The En'owkin Journal of First North American Peoples*, Vol. IV, Theytus Books. Penticton.

Creation

IT Geography

When we leave our body,
the sound is so potent
it cracks open the stars
and our momentum ricochets around.

Then *fichik heli*, streams of radiance
shoot across the darkness and we speed up motion.
Our mind is space unbounded
everywhere we are, everything is.

Time becomes a deep breath,
a pause in the telling
as rivers of ash collide with memory.
And for us nothing will ever be over and done with.

Allahe.

We circle the heavens.
Then one day we create something unexpected.
A pulse, a hot flash.
And it flows through the veins of space.

Allahe.

We blush
and tiny beads of perspiration
form on the brows of heaven
reflecting light.

Allahe.

We are hot, we say!
Soon we spasm in a spiral of passion,
mounting and arching, expanding, and contracting
we expel volumes of water the size of blue green oceans.

Allahe.

We are *born.*

Evidence of Red

First, night opened out
Bodies took root from rotting salt
and seawater into evidence of red life.
Relentless waves pumped tidal air
into a single heartbeat.

In the pulp of shadow and space,
water sucked our people from sleep.
That's how it all began. At least
that's all we can remember to tell.
It began with water and heartbeat.

In minutes we tunneled through
corn woman's navel into tinges
of moist red men and women.
Yawning, we collected our chins,
knees, breasts, and sure-footed determination.

A few thousand years before
Moses parted the Red Sea, and the
God with three heads was born in the Middle East,
the Choctaw people danced
our homeland infra red.

Finally when the stranger's arms
reached to strangle the West,
Grandmother eavesdropped
on the three-faced deity
who said that chaos was coming.

When he puckered his lips and tried to kiss her
she made it rain on him.
"Maybe you've forgotten
you were born of water and women,"
she said, walking away laughing.

Hashi mi Mali

I

Each morning, *Hashi*, the stark red creator rises,
swelling,
she passes over the ground,
spilling a drop or two of her blood
which grows the corn and the people. *Okla* are we.
Naked, she goes down on us,
her flaming hair burns us brown.
Finally, in the month of *Tek Inhashi*, the Sun of Women,
when we are navel deep in red sumac,
we cut the leaves and smoke to her success.
Sing her praises.
Hashi won't forget.

II

When *Ohoyo Ikbi* pulled
freshly made *Chahta Okla*
out of her red thighs,
we were very wet, so
one-by-one,
she stacked us
on the mound,
and *Hashi* kissed our
bodies with her morning lips
and painted our faces with afternoon fire,
and in the month of *Hash Hoponi*, the Sun of Cooking,
We were made.

III

It is said that
once-a-month warriors can kill a thing with spit.
So when the soldiers came,
our mothers stood on the tops of the
ramparts and made the *Tashka* call
urging their men on.
Whirling their tongues and hatchets in rhythm,
they pulled red water and fire from their bodies
and covered their chests with bullet-proof blood.
When it was over, they made a fire bed on the prairie that
blew across the people like a storm.
Melded our souls with iron.

IIII

And in the month of *Hash Mali*, the Sun of Wind,
We listen for the voices
that still urge us on
At sunrise.

The Unknown Women

Stage Directions: (Minimal staging and props. All action takes place on an empty dark stage. Use spot lighting to highlight actors during narration.)

FIRST CHARACTER — THE SPIRIT

From the landscape of imagination,
I noiselessly dream beneath clouds
illuminated like bleach on blue silk
And in a vision
I am told to create a poem
to live inside of.

There is breath
Inhaling past and present forms everything—
Tender shoots of cosmic energy
aim their sperm into the sun
and she spasms
launching a pulpy sweet body.

I become irresistible in a dress
Made of *Fichik isi nula sil h hi*
Brilliant white stars.
Serene, yet steamy,
I use the light coming from inside me to attract attention.
Something thrives and mounts the mist

Silhouetted insinuations
we form people,
Things with underpinnings.
Purpose.
All properties that are necessary,
but not sufficient to define.

What they will say is
my poem is *Anuk la mampa.*
Anuk la mampa
the power of thought
represented as food.
Are you surprised?

Look beyond me. At us. It. This moment. Can you see what just
happened? Copper masks made by my children appear in the Field
Museum's case. They rest in the future—from the past—folded
together pinioned to a web of metallic shadows. *Huh,* the power of
poetry! I feel just like William Shakespeare will feel in a distant
moment, from my words, generations of artists are born.

Music Directions: (A refrain that is the signature melody for FIRST
CHARACTER — THE SPIRIT.*)*

I begin to think of myself as a cosmic dress.
Here are my underpinnings:

Ho tan tona—"She who seeks—goes along and gets there."
Be-ia—ya e-e- hona—(Baiyillihona) "She who follows another and
    gets there."
Ho tima—"She who seeks and gives advice."
Mantema—"To go and carry or deliver something sacred or
    particular."
Wak a ya tema (Wakayatima) "Get up and deliver it."

I deliver myself unto you now. My intent is breath and mind, the
power of thought represented as food. *Anuk la mampa.* I AM the one
you long for.

Sound Directions: (Use a sound to evoke Ohoyo Chish-Ba Osh. THE
UNKNOWN WOMAN.*)*

Ohoyo Chish-Ba Osh. THE UNKNOWN WOMAN

It has been my experience that the most intimate thing we do, we accomplish with haste.

This is true for me, as well.
I came in haste.
I am *Ohoyo Chish-Ba Osh*, The Unknown Woman. I begin my story in the middle. . . .

It was a time of white moons:

Two of my people are camped for the night in the swamps along the river *Ali Bamu*. They hunger and eat the carcasses of birds. Pitiful, they need me for strength. As the two warriors listen to the gloomy sounds of water lapping against the black muddy shore, they cry out for longing, the noun, I mean, *Na Bano*, and like an illuminating shadow I appear to the Choctaw hunters.

Loosely clad in the cool white mist, I wear a wreath of fragrant flowers in my hair and beckon for them to approach. It is then I fall to my knees and produce a sound I will never again utter as *Ohoyo Chish-Ba Osh*.
With my own hands
I slay all reason
tear out my hair
and tassel the four directions with my seed.
The warriors inhale me. I am mercy in their mouths.
I become Corn Woman.
And I am mercy in their mouths.

Music Directions: Fade out music.

Ohoyo Chish-Ba Osh. THE UNKNOWN WOMAN

People have speculated about my life, but the truth is, I was a romantic, bred for giving. "In the beginning" I will say, "I desired to be a Host." A provider. Savior of the World. Being a host is an imprecise calling, I know, and a dangerous one. I will not tell it all, just the parts I want to giveaway.

Sound Directions: The sound of shaking shells beneath narration.

Corn is grown in more countries in the world than any other food crop, And *Yakni Achukma* exports more corn than any other land in the world. I suppose I am fully realized now. Did you know that in Romania I am boiled with potatoes to make a mush—and that the Romanians say I am their traditional food? In Cairo Egypt, I am the same breakfast cereal as in Battle Creek, Michigan. However the Turks, always the bossy ones, claim I originated in their homelands, but it's their custom to allege that all things come from Turkia and the Ottoman Empire.

After my first dream, I went into the protective Earth. Out of boredom I sometimes created a world for myself that was full of desire. I had no way of knowing that it was wrong to covet a precarious existence. For instance, when a rainbow landed on my belly I tried to propel myself toward the arch—and it singed the silk of my vulva. As a result, I will turn all the shades of the rainbow during growing season. For a while I was a little embarrassed by this and sank deeper into the soil until the rains came and I had trouble breathing. Naked, I twisted upward and a friendly worm gave me the final push. Afterwards, I began to grow easily in sunlight.

Then one day there came a small boy, lean, not by choice but by circumstance. "I am looking for a host," he says to no one in particular. He wears the same dirty clothes he wore when he arrived He represents the Old World well, and like the Old World, he refuses to wash or braid his colorless, lifeless, hair. In fact, the only thing that does change about him is his expression. In time, his young body with its pallid flat cheeks will harden to stone.

"I will find the host," he says persistently.

"But I am here for everyone." I answer. "See my praying rows of corn."

He doesn't see anything, but metal and machinery. Eventually, a Hummer races toward him squealing its tires past generations of my people. The Legendary H1. The Old World freezes, blinded by high beams and technology, and in an instant, the boy leaps off the road. The Hummer stops to gas up on ethanol, a mixture made of corn and oil, then accelerates along a dark road made by the God of Tourists.

In the twinkling of an eye another earnest white man appears, this one being a kind of evolved- God-himself. He says, being God isn't a job so much as second nature. No fixed rules except this: Both hands get used in the taking. Imagine, he says, as far as the eye can see miles and miles of empty, but gleaming red earth. By day, it's Egypt and the Arabian Desert, by night, Monument Valley where the Navajos dress like Apaches. Like you, he says, whatever I visualize comes true.

After a time we begin to breathe like one person, the same heartbeat, the same hunger. *Na Bano.* We sleep side-by-side, but never touch. His God has told him that our union will never yield anything, not even relief. So when we do it, we do it apart. I am easily aroused and easily satisfied and each kernel I produce represents an orgasm. He is repulsed by my sex, but likes to fondle my ears—finally he rips them off one-by-one, my drying ears with their cooking smells. He weaves them into a wreath he will wear around his neck to fertility parades.

See the suspended animation behind his eyes as he sends in the cows to gorge on my flesh and blood. It seems everything comes down to my eradication. No, not eradication, my use as a shape changer. What an erotic disaster I have become.

I am dragged against my will through a million fields of those who purposely deform my body. Blind. Deaf. Friendless. Sometimes I am tortured with acids that swell my body beyond grace. Eventually, the son of God sends Agronomists disguised as Angels to study me. They take field trips and write exhaustive notes about their experiences with corn. I am no longer beautiful, nor represented as food for thought.

I am corn whiskey
Mother's milk to the addicted.
Because of me,
my first children
are wizened at my breasts.
Suckled to death.

See the nitrate plow tilling the rivers and waterways.
My poem swerves and takes a mean curve
forming a pattern of struggle.
Watchful geese
shrouded in my mist
wait for blessings
to surface as dead fish.
Baby alligators patiently stand guard
in the narrow bayous where I came down as food.
I warn you—someday they will grow into warriors on a killing
        spree.
What has happened to my poetic vision?

I am completely blue now.
For Greeks,
change meant their Gods became
intellectual concepts.
Psyche, Venus, Ego, Mercury.
I wonder if this has already happened to me?
Is Corn Woman a concept? *Huh!*
Never real. A myth. A commodity?
Blue Corn Chips.
White Corn Chips?
Red again.
I am a buck a bag in some grocery markers.

And you claim you never devour anything with a face
Shame on you Mary Tyler Moore!
Everything is alive
Everything is past
Present
Future
Something endures.
And I tell you now
 I dreamed the vision that is you.
And I wait.

RED WOMAN

Stage Directions: (She enters the stage in a huff carrying a set of books marked "Indian" in large letters. Plops them on a small square table.)

Go ahead ask me. Subjects are on the table, but I don't think you'll find any answers.

(Use sarcastic voice)

She said, everything is related
Everything is past and present
Everything is future
Something survives and endures, huh?

God damn her, I hate that New Age shit!
Who does she think she is?

Stage Directions: (Ohoyo Chish-Ba Osh. THE UNKNOWN WOMAN
*steps into the second spotlight. She appears soulful and sad as she stares
at her ancestor, Red Woman. She says nothing.)*

RED WOMAN

I'll grant you, she has a habit of being an enigmatic as hell. She loves
to answer questions with questions, and she dismisses her
enormous influence with *"huh,"* as if she didn't know it. I'll tell you
right now, if she is THE CORN WOMAN, I'm THE Little Red Riding
Hood.

Stage Directions: (Ohoyo Chish-Ba Osh. THE UNKNOWN WOMAN
holds up a sign that says, LITTLE RED RIDING HOOD WAS AN INDIAN.)

RED WOMAN

Stage Directions: (She sees the sign.)

If she's not a seething mass of contradictions I don't know what is.
She's always doing shit like this.

(Pause)

She once said, "I'm distrustful of ethnographers like John Swanton or even John Neihardt so that makes me very guarded with my stories." Despite her voice, low and smooth as satin, her words come in *rat-a-tat* stream of nervous energy. Is Corn Woman the nervous type? I don't think so.

Stage Directions: (Ohoyo Chish-Ba Osh. THE UNKNOWN WOMAN *holds up another sign that says, "I am too nervous."*)

RED WOMAN

Stage Directions: (She ignores the sign.)

She says, "Authors tend to get it all wrong. Really, you shouldn't believe everything you read." Well, listen honey, Indians no longer tell stories, not new ones anyway, so the books are all we have.

Personally I think she's just on a mission to let you know she isn't certifiable. That is weird, in and of itself, since she's just spent the last fifteen minutes letting you know how weird she is. Explaining how she tore her own hair out of her scalp, turned her orgasms into kernels of corn, and then there was the time—not too long ago—when she said she liked to wear men's underwear. Talk about kinky. And now she wants you to know all that stuff isn't that strange if you think about it—or better yet, if you don't think about it.

Sure, she likes the attention an awful lot—and I'll grant you she has a kind of strange intensity you don't normally see after high school. But describing herself as Corn Woman, full of desire, and "being completely blue," Oh please. I know for a fact that she eats corn on the cob, and corn tortillas. So she can't be the reincarnation of Corn Woman. One does not eat one's self.

Stage Directions: (Ohoyo Chish-Ba Osh. THE UNKNOWN WOMAN *pulls out a bag of corn chips and eats one. Spotlight fades.)*

Music (Striking Sticks)

CHOCTAW WOMAN

I'll tell you what I know—one Red woman to another:

Over the centuries, Choctaws and other Red People have seemed to produce only one idea: the freedom to create. A long time ago a Choctaw would leave behind every extraneous comfort and go to live in the swamp— to dream.

Perhaps we deserved the reputation we gained for this kind of escapism. "Primitive." The idea of absolute zero is purely Choctaw. It made us entirely useless as builders of empires, but incalculable in spirit. The ethnographers, anthropologists, and historians, even New Agers who've tried to discover the meaning of being Native, or Indigenous, or Choctaw have found nothing to document, but a longing to know more.

Now here is all you need to know!

Stage Directions: (The Southeastern Ceremonial symbol of the Hand should appear in spotlights lights, blue, red, yellow, green, all around the stage.)

Stage Directions: (CHOCTAW WOMAN gestures with her hands.)

Here is the power! The vision. And it grows under your fingernails, crawls up your sleeves and enters . . . You.

Stage Directions: (Spotlight on the four women as they change places and costumes onstage.)

RED WOMAN

How could I have been so foolish to stop believing in the power of story?

Stage Directions: (Characters hold hands.)

RED WOMAN

This is the season when constellations turn—and spring arrives.

We are the daughters (and sons) of creation.
We are Food for thought.
We carry the old—all of us,
And in return for this gift, we create the new stories.

Ho tan tona—"She who seeks—goes along and gets there."
Be-ia—ya e-e- hona—(Baiyillihona) "She who follows another and gets there."
Ho tima—"She who seeks and gives advice."
Mantema—"To go and carry or deliver something sacred or particular."
Wak a ya tema (Wakayatima) "Get up and deliver it."

Stage Directions: (Characters chant together.)

What are you waiting for? Get up and deliver the stories. They are powerful monologues. They create people and author tribes.

Look way beyond us—what do you see?

Stage Directions: (Audience holds hands and chant together. "The Beginning.")

Music Directions: (End with refrain that is the signature melody for FIRST CHARACTER — THE SPIRIT.*)*

Chaos

The Chaos of Angels

When the Upper and Lower Worlds collide in the Between World, there is a reaction in This World. Our ancestors called it, *Huksuba*. Today we say chaos.

Huksuba, or chaos occurs when Indians and Non-Indians bang their heads together in search of cross-cultural understanding. The sound is often a dull thud, and the lesson leaves us all with a bad headache.

First there is the 2 am heartbeat. The sound of my own breathing keeps me from sleep. I leave my bed for the comfort of the heated outdoor swimming pool, and the relentless motion of water

In New Orleans, during February, delicate lukewarm rain falls. Fog exists. The night sky, neon and purple fire, compete for the senses.

In the central courtyard of the old world hotel, green French shutters hang on eighteenth century windows. A black woman peers from behind a shuttered window. She stares at me floating alone in the heated outdoor pool.

This gilded black figure throws a red swatch of cloth tied with chicken feathers out the window. The cloth flies away.

I continue in silence, pretending to ignore the tease. Intrigued only by steaming water. Intimate with my own nakedness.

Again, there is a summons. A moment of red. A moment of deafness, and a crowless rooster flies from the arms of the black woman. She is craving attention. She will get it. Enough is enough.

Onto the courtyard with much ado, march green-footed doormen, with blue-tattooed mouths. Heartbeat for heartbeat, two-by-two, they are turtles in disguise.

Ancient ones out of the mud of the Mississippi River, they stand ready and watching over me. They've come to remind her that the conquering hordes only thought the Choctaw camps were abandoned and the dogs were mute, and the stains on their hands, red-colored and blue, were sweet scent.

"After all," I whisper aloud. "Have you ever seen what a turtle does to the reckless fowl who lands in its water space?"

Soon the black woman departs, laughing. The joke is on her.

The next day, I catch a flight out of New Orleans bound for Dallas, Texas. On the plane, a beautiful Haitian flight attendant offers me a strong red drink. Red again.

Her voice is lilting and mysterious. She cups her hands around my hands when she gives me the red drink. I swallow it without breathing.

In New Orleans, everyone I know is drunk fifty-percent of the time. I myself am drunk fifty-percent of the time. Naw'lins people say "likkah" for liquor. Absolut for vodka.

I pass out thinking about the smoothness of the Haitian woman's hands and how her long, slender fingers remind me of the ancient Jean Baptiste Le Moyne Sieur de Bienville. His hands are said to have helped shape the "New World."

Bienville still roams the streets of New Orleans, the city he platted out of swampland in 1718. I saw him one night on d'Iberville Street in the French Quarter. Ears back, eyes rolling in his head, he more resembled a tree frog hugging a lamppost than a jazzman fingering a saxophone. But it was him.

My Choctaw ancestor called Bienville, *Filanchi*, which is short for "Our Frenchman, the Nail Bitter." They liked him, although he was nervous and could never take a joke. The first time they invited him for dinner he started making problems that have continued until now.

Back in the old days, dining with the tribe was not at all like having dinner with your next-door neighbor. No, Choctaw dinners were meant to be experienced. These weeklong, elaborately arranged soirées were evenings of collective communication. Dinner guest were always selected carefully, juxtaposing good jokers with good listeners. Guests were also expected to report in great detail about other tribal groups, gossip being one of our favorite sports. However, what Bienville did before the meal began was to toss some third rate glass beads on the ground and ask if my relatives would trade them for "un morceau de terre." (A morsel of land somewhere.)

This glitch in decorum put a damper on the cross-cultural understanding between the French and Choctaw peoples. Such was this breach of etiquette that my relatives decided to have some fun with him.

"You want us to exchange land for these flimsy discount beads? What kind of chicanery are you trying to pull on *vos amis les sauvages.*" (Your friends, the savages?)

"*Ne vendez pas le peau de l'ours avant de l'avoir tuee.*" Do not sell the bearskin before you've killed the bear." "*N'est pas, mon ami?*" (My grandmother loved to mock his speech.)

"Besides," she continued, "the English traders are giving us some terrific deals on black powder muskets." (You may or may not remember that the rivalry between the French and the English traders in the early eighteenth century was at a fever pitch at this time.)

At this point Bienville's expression underwent a complete and violent change. He started in on my relatives and would not let up.

"When zee English and your friends, zee Chickasaws, were beating the shish kebob out of you in 1702, who came in with zee foreign policy muscle to save your corn, your potatoes, your tomatoes, your pumpkins, your beans, and your yellow-squashed asses? Just who?" shouted the little Frenchmen with confidence.

Bienville pointed to my relatives seated before him he continued. "Just who used zheir swag to provide you with weapons and gun powder, interest free? Tell me? Any one of you who zhinks it was zee English, raise your hands!

"Ah-ha, no takers! Bon. We are getting somewhere. Just who . . ."

My grandmother near went deaf from listening to this tirade. Before Filanchi could tune-up for another crybaby episode she called together a special session of all the men and women to decide what to do with him. Some wanted to kill him right on the spot, others thought of torture. Elder heads prevailed and they decided to have some fun with him. Sort of. They traded him the swampland that belonged to our cousins, the Bayougoulas. That's right. Swampland.

In return, my relatives received some first rate axes, some metal pots, and a dozen used musket rifles. They also took the flimsy glass beads off his hands. When my relatives told the Bayogoulas what happened, they all went four-paws-up laughing because the land that had been traded was a huge flood plain. Six months out of every year it was knee deep in water, snakes and alligators. Nowhere were there more mosquitoes than on that piece of land. Most days of the year the air was so thick with mosquitoes that you couldn't distinguish one person from another ten paces away.

Naturally my relatives shared the trade goods with the Bayougoulas and the whole wheedling affair was largely forgotten by both peoples. Then one afternoon a group of Choctaws were tramping though the area and stumbled across Filanchi and his soldiers, now get this, camping in two feet of water. Imagine their surprise. My grandfather called to him from higher ground. (He was not an imbecile, after all.)

"*Filanchi*, what are you doing down there?"

Well, Bienville started in on Grandfather just like he had my grandmother. He was flailing his hands like a lunatic and babbling on and on. The gist of his harangue, and I hope I'm not misquoting him, was that the land was his. The end.

"*Messieurs Chahtas*, as you remember, I have traded for zeese land fair and square, and by our Holy Reverend Father, I will defend it to zee death."

Filanchi then went on to say that the bayous had overflowed so furiously that he and his men had been four months in waist high water. My grandfather had to turn away to keep from laughing himself silly.

Filanchi then staggered. "You're *femmes* assured me zhat zeese place was never inundated. Look at zeese mess! I don't understand? Zeese is all your fault."

Poor thing. He could barely see to curse my grandfather because the mosquitoes had stung him in both eyes, and he had tried to cover his swollen face with a sort of bandage-like-thing. It was in this sad moment that we realized the truth of the matter. Our Frenchman, The Nail Biter, did not have all his oars in the water. Since advice is the most repulsive of all faults, showing disrespect for the feathers of common sense in others, my relatives left him there soaked to the skin, standing in the middle of "New France." And it wasn't until much later that we realized the joke was on us.

Now, as I have said into eternity, there was a continual rhythm of give and take among Indian tribes in the southeast. We gave, they gave. That's how things had been done for about 2,000 years, until Filanchi showed up. I'm not kidding; no one had ever wanted land. Forever. This was an anomaly. This changed all rules of government-to-government cooperation. We had no idea how to proceed.

Oh, I take that back. My relatives had come across this kind of thing before. Grandmother loved to tell the story about some foreign tribe, I think they were from Spain or Portugal. Well anyway, they ventured into our territory and just demanded all the tribe's gold. Choctaws never had gold. Not really. Occasionally they could trade for it down South, but my relatives never found gold to be particularly useful. However, these spiritual shoppers would not take no for an answer. First they begged, pestered, then threatened:

"O nos dais el maldito oro, o os cortamos el cuello!"

Finally our men gave in. They heated up what little gold they had into a fiery red liquid and poured it down the tourist's throats.

As I chuckle to myself about Grandmother's story, I lose my concentration. I believe I am back at my writing desk, working on another chapter of my novel, or filming a scene of an avant-garde video I want to produce. But my mind is in chaos. Suddenly, Bienville steps into my brain with his saxophone hooked on his neck chain. He begins playing a little melody, but he stops long enough to deliver narration into an invisible microphone:

"It is morning. A young woman is window shopping in zee French Quarter. In zee background zhere are other stores, other shops, but zhey are out of focus. Zhere are other people milling around, but zhey are in zee background and blurry.

"*La femme* stops in front of a large storefront window. She wears a white raincoat and carries a white plastic umbrella.

"Our heroine stares into the bedroom shop window. She sees zhere are two intertwined, faceless figures lying on zee bed. The figures are covered completely by white cotton sheets and beneath the sheets zhey are wearing white full-body stockings. The white rain woman believes zhey are two murdered corpses, until zhey begin coupling as if by an automated timer."

He plays another riff on his saxophone, then continues his soliloquy:

"Zee stocking people begin to make love. One tenderly mounts zee other. Zhey hunch slowly in heartbeat rhythm. The lover's faces and hair color remain anonymous to our heroine, her breathing quickens and she wets her lips with her tongue and chants in sync with the rhythmic lovers, fuck me. Fuck me!"

"Oh God, zeese is good!" says Bienville.

"Help," I holler and sit straight up in my seat.

I'm confused. Maybe I'm drunk? Just as I think I've come to my senses someone shakes me awake.

IT looks like a bug-eyed man, with thick wide lips, wearing cowboy clothes and an obnoxious leather belt with the capital letters B-u-l-l etched across the silver buckle.

"Are you practicing safe sex, gal? Holy Cow. Look out the window. The earth is much bigger than I guessed. Wait until Grandmother hears about this"

I slap myself in the face, but this thing is still seated next to me.

"Do I know you?" I ask. "And what do you mean was I practicing safe sex?"

"Of course you know me. But I don't know what I mean. Not anymore. Thoughts just pop in my head. I guess it's because you were thinking about sex and water, and power. I just say what pops in my head.

"Rivvit, rivvit . . . . Oops."

The thing cups its slender hands over its mouth and shyly looks at me. Then it chatters on like I'm an old friend. It isn't even speaking a language, although it is mimicking a language. Every few phrases are in English, but they're gibberish.

"You know," it says, "I think cats and alligators are related. They have those same funny eyes. Slanted pupils. And, you know alligators and birds are related. Hollow bones. I think cats could fly once upon a time. You know how they're always climbing trees and they don't mind when you throw them off buildings. Wow! Look down zhere. Is that a lake?"

"Rivvit, rivvit . . . . . . Uh-hum, excuse me."

I am alive. I'm flying in an airplane somewhere over Louisiana and Texas. However, judging from the thing's obsession with cats, I realize I'm staring at an ancient French frog, a holdover from last night's spirit world rivalry.

You see, cats held great mystery to the eighteenth-century French people. Cats appealed to poets like Baudelaire, and yet to the citizens of Aix-en-Provence, cats were used like baseballs before cheering crowds as they smacked kitten and tomcat alike into the nearest wall. But that's not the worst of it. They also ate their brains when they wanted to be invisible, provided the gray matter was still hot.

The French also made a mixed drink from cat feces and red wine that they called a tonic for colic. (And they called Indians, *les sauvages*.)

It was the French who coined the phrase, "Patient as a cat whose paws are being grilled." They also believed that cats were witches in disguise, so brave Frenchmen and women devised remedies to save themselves from danger by maiming, "Kitty-kitty."

They cut kitty's tails, clipped kitty's ears, smashed kitty's legs, tore or burned kitty's fur, and hanged kitty – until almost dead. The thinking in France, at the time, was that a mutilated housecat would be too embarrassed to walk into a church and cast a spell. Go figure?

The cat was also symbolic of 'Old World' sexual culture: Le chat, la chatte, le minet, roughly translates into the English expression for 'pussy.' If a Frenchman petted a kitten, he would have success in courting a mate. If a Frenchwoman stepped on a cat's tail she would not get her man.

Cats were strictly an 'Old World' thing. So were barnyard chickens. Both were foreign imports to the 'New World.' I am proud to say that American Indians never ate cats. We preferred deer, bear, buffalo, corn, beans, squash, pumpkins, potatoes, onions, tomatoes, chocolate, pecans, and of course, the turkey. As far as the Choctaws were concerned, chickens were entirely too small to satisfy serious Choctaw diners.

After looking more closely at the French frog seated next to me, I recognized "IT" for whom it was. Bienville, that big phony, was disguised as a bullfrog. I glance around the cabin for the Haitian flight attendant, knowing she's in on this nightmare, but she's nowhere to be found.

Now he starts in on me, just like he had Grandmother. "You know I like flying," he says coyly. "Of course, this can't compare to riding in a red, 1963 Ford Galaxy convertible with the top down listening to Nancy Sinatra sing, 'These Boots Are Made For Walking.'

"I love my cowboy boots. Whaddaya think of 'em?

"I sing myself electronic!

"You know why Sitting Bull was a star? It was because he had a good public relations man.

"Reality is a rubber band you can pull in any direction."

I clinched my fists and scream. "Shut up, shut up, shut up. I want you to shut up and go away. What do you want? Who sent you?"

A blonde flight attendant walks past us, and we both smile at her as if nothing is wrong. He looks away, rueful and uneasy. He nervously bites a loose fingernail. Finally, he pulls his wide lips together, until his mouth resembles an egg. "You should have remembered that for every action there is a reaction. I don't know how much that vulgar display of alchemy cost you last night when you were in the swimming pool. But I think you lost Grandmother's respect. She said you always act like 'Puss 'n Boots'."

"My grandmother told you no such thing. If you don't stop lying I'm going to put you in a mayonnaise jar and screw the lid on tight."

My threat has little impact. The banter stops when he pulls a tiny saxophone from underneath his seat and begins playing *Beautiful Dreamer* by Stephen Foster. And I closed my eyes and try to dream him away.

The memories that will come back to me when I dream are so far removed by generations that the pain of them is no longer present. They roll forward like silent videos of something that happened, not to me, not to my bones that inhabit these memories, but to the part of me they are.

My first memories are of complete darkness. You would not call them memories, but something given by blood from her, while she still carried me in her body.

First, there is the sound of water and heartbeat.
A call from the Upper World to the Lower World.
Chahtas crawled up through the mud of the Nanih Waiya, and into the sun's light. We washed ourselves off and combed our long hairs.

Some of us lived like crayfish.
Some of us lived like turtles.
Some of us lived like coiled snakes end to end.
Some of us lived like people.

We danced, prayed, practiced our songs, learned to hunt, and grew the tall green corn that balanced our lives for 2000 years before the whites forcibly removed us to Oklahoma. After the long walk on the trail of bad memories to Indian Territory, our past experiences seemed to change us.

I can see my relatives now, walking west at sunset. Fireballs are bursting around their heads. Then my grandmother falls down. Something is wrong.

"Get up, Grandmother, get up." I pull at her shoulders but she doesn't move. "Somebody help us."

Suddenly, I am running. In the next moment, someone shakes me awake. The frog has disappeared, but the woman from the hotel courtyard is sitting next to me.

"You called?" she asked. "Haven't you forgotten that the French took some of your relatives to Haiti where they made a new home there. How could you forget that we are sisters? Maybe the joke is on you, after all?

I start to laugh at myself.

"Are you finished with me?" I ask, trying to hide my embarrassment.

"Not yet," she answers. "Come with me."

I follow her to the first class section of the plane. Sitting in the front row is Grandmother watching, "Star Wars" on the big screen. When she turns to look at me, her warm smile pulls me into the seat next to her.

"I love this movie, don't you?" she whispers. "Darth Vader wears such wonderful headgear."

"Grandmother, what are you doing here?" I ask.

"First, she played a joke," she says, pointing with her lips at my sister standing in the aisle. "Then you forgot your sense of humor, and now I'm finishing the joke. We all must work hand in hand. Besides it was time for Bienville to return to his group. Enough's enough. *Shu-u-sh-h*, this is where they blow the Death Star to pieces," she says.

I look at her with wonder. "Grandmother, I don't know what to think about anything anymore."

She turns from the movie and continues whispering. "Never forget we are all alive! All people, all animals, all living things; and what you do here affects all of us everywhere. What we do affects you, too."

She pats my face and begins talking in a normal voice. "Our ancestors survived wars, the Europeans, diseases, and removal from our homelands. Now, my group, which is many generations older than your group, is learning how to survive the chaos of all these ethnocentric angels. It's what we've started to call, "a cross-cultural afterlife, living challenge."

She smiles and says, "It beats banging our heads together."

With that, she grabs my sister's hand and my hand, and the three of us watch Darth Vader alone zooming across the universe in a tiny spaceship. In the tribal ethos, being isolated from one's relatives is the worst horror we can imagine, so we hold each other tight in the scary parts and wonder what will happen next.

How My Fever Broke

Homage to Richard Wright's "How my Fever Left"

I can still hear him
Calling night out of the bed
Calling my name.
My necklace, hot, like my forehead
Wake up, he says.
His voice is pianissimo,
a musical instrument.
I respond to his softness.
His sensitive fingers. His pianissimo.
And again I try to remember what it was like.

Using my narrator's voice, I must say something about the epidemic of 1918 that killed twenty-five percent of the American population. It was foreign, and unknown like all epidemics and pathogens that came to the New World killing the most beautiful in its path.

Both Iva and John Hoggatt, my grandparents contracted the 1918 flu, along with so many others around Stonewall, Oklahoma. Between September and October of 1918, 500,000 died in the United States. The flu hit in Southeastern Oklahoma in October.

My grandparents fell ill on a Friday in their home on Owl Creek. First, they had headaches. Then their eyes burned. An hour or so later, they ran a high fever. Within two hours their faces developed brown or bluish spots and swelled up. Grandfather, although only 28 at the time, began to cough blood. The bleeding continued and his lungs fill up with blood.

When John began to bleed uncontrollably, his father sent for the doctor who was already knee-deep in dying people all over the county. The doctor never arrived. John's sisters, Euda and Macey, and Grandpa Hoggatt tried to put cotton plugs in John's nose to stop the bleeding, but he drown in his own blood. It only took a day and a half. Iva, my grandmother, was lying beside him and unconscious. When she rallied, she gave Euda, her sister-in-law, instructions on how to raise her daughter because she was certain she too would die.

Euda was John's youngest sister who would later run off and join the circus. We have pictures of Euda dressed up in feathers and leather like an Indian princess. It was part of her circus costume.

John Hoggatt's friend, Lon Valentine Cecil, laid John out in a pine box coffin. "Laid him out," is an old-timer's term meaning, Lon Cecil cleaned John Hoggatt's body, dressed him in his Sunday suit, then helped bury him. Lon Cecil would later become my grandfather, but that is another story.

After Iva recovered, she was broke and without anyone to work her farm. She and her daughter, my mother, went to live with Uncle Carroll. Iva hired herself out as a housekeeper. She said she was accountable to Uncle Carroll's no-account wife. Iva was paid $12.00 per year, or a dollar a month, which was not enough to keep her farm going. She lost everything, and eventually married Lon Cecil.

The flu is at the door,
coming from the east
blowing westward.
Feel my forehead
open my nightshirt,
but before you do,
remove the necklace
then give me your mouth.

Tonight our dream tastes blue,
naked, we're old lovers
curled up in a cross-fire.
Even the rooster that crows
next to the bedroom is forlorn

I still hear him calling
night out of our bed
Wake up.
It's 3 am.

Oh don't let me

The Red Wars

I can catch all the flies for you, Mama. I'll go to the flies' nest.
— RANDY CRAIG, 1977

PART I

He has long beautiful braids. Clear skin. He does not smoke
cigarettes. A slender man who looks to be about twenty-five. Maybe
thirty. He is wearing a navy blue sport coat. Tight fitting, new 501s.
Expensive boots. I smell him. He's interesting. He is Sioux.

Thunderhawk is not from Oklahoma.
He carries a leather briefcase with beading on it. I think he must
    be rich.
He's raising money to help get Dennis Banks out of jail. He is in
    a hurry.
It is the early 1970s. I'm working at the office of the ACLU.
A red-haired woman in the next room is raising money for AIM.
She's telephoning the Oklahoma City liberals.
We know it won't take long.

He paces.

We stare past each other, never capturing gazes,
never out of sight of one another.
His scent envelops me.
He touches me with his scent.
He seduces me with his scent.
I am drunk with his scent.
He asks if I am Indian. I say Choctaw.

"Of course," he says.

Often I think of the image of myself that day.
I am young with long straight hair
and I do it to myself every day.

Many times a day.
Alone in the mornings.
During my bath.
Alone at night.

I can do it while sitting at my typewriter without moving.
It is the image I delight in.
The image I remember best. Secretive and silent. A holdover from home. No one guesses what goes on with the timid little receptionist.
No one guesses what goes on with Indians when they're alone.
The fights, the 49s. Unspoken piety, unspoken wild.
No one can know just by looking.

Thunderhawk knows of these things and ignores them.
He moves closer to my desk.
He talks on.
He tells me I should join AIM and help build a better tomorrow for Indians. He shows me a map where the new Indian Nation will be established.
It will be carved out of New Mexico.
All Indians can move there.

He tells me AIM is going to get a seat on the United Nations.
He says the seat will be sponsored by Norway.

Thunderhawk whispers about a stash of machine guns and weapons in the desert. He says Indians are going to make the United States take notice.
He says Indians will get a separate nation, one way of the other.
He reminds me of a black and white movie, I've just seen on the late show. A drama. An American couple adopts a young boy from Germany after WWII. The boy has been brainwashed by the Nazis and rails at everyone in the movie. It's called *Tomorrow the World*.

Thunderhawk tells me I should get involved.
"Come smoke with me, tonight. What are you doing here?
Join us. Tomorrow, come with me.
I will teach you things."

I tell him I have two babies I must raise.
He says they will be taken care of too.
I tell him I'm a student earning credit by working for the ACLU
and when I get my degree I will work as a tribal lawyer.

"Of course," He says.

Thunderhawk dismisses me, and goes in and out of the next
        room.
He's checking the redhead's progress.
When it's time to leave, he gives me an address and asks me to
change my mind. He touches my hands. I say nothing. He calls me
"Choctaw," then braces himself and turns away.
At 6 p.m. I call the babysitter. I will be home in time to cook
        dinner.
I put the phone down and smell the back of my hand.

PART II

We meet at a burial for an estranged skull.
He is holding a bundle of sage and chanting
for the dead in a language I don't understand.
I'm a reporter for the *Dallas Morning News*.

I am there to see what this is all about.
He wears a ribbon shirt and sunglasses.
His gray hair is long and braided on the nape of the neck.
He is a chain smoker.

Someone in the background calls him "Chief."
I ask him what tribe he is?
He says he's part Dakota, part Navajo.
He says he was raised in New York City.

"Of course," I say.

He invites me to his home.
I am eager to learn why he is called Chief.
And, I'm hungry to be with Indians—
Indians out of costume.

California Red Wing is the Chief of an Indian non-profit
corporation. He calls himself a man of medicine. He says he
conducts sweats and ceremonies and has learned the prayers from
a medicine man
who lives on a South Dakota Reservation.

California Red Wing says there's another group of Indians in Dallas
similar to his not-for-profit group. He says they're fighting him.
He tells me they are no good and only in it for the money.
He says his group and the Dallas group each want
the Texas Sesquicentennial Commission in Austin
to proclaim them the only Indian no-profit organization of
        Texas.
California Red Wing says his group will fight until the bitter
        end.

I tell him I don't understand.
He says things are different in Texas, than in Oklahoma.
He says they can let you in or keep you out.
I ask who is they?

The telephone rings. A woman has been killed in Lake Worth, Texas.
Someone asks California Red Wing to bury her the Indian way. He

agrees. He hangs up. He says his heart is heavy. He says the girl was only seventeen and the only black member of his non-profit corporations.
He tells me she was part Indian on her mother's side.

I say nothing. I show no emotion. It's a learned thing.
I look at California Red Wing.
He still wears sunglasses.
I leave and drive to the nearest bar.

PART III

He is standing at the bar. Dark blue shirt, unbuttoned to the
       third button.
His skins is tanned dark red. Flat-top hair.
His neck skin is micro-pitted like the skin of a Winesap apple.
His name is Jim or Jack. I will call him Jim-Jack.

We're at a Country Club in West Columbia, Texas.
We are being introduced because he is said to be Indian of some
       stripe.
He says he builds houses and introduces me to his wife, Betty or
       Margaret.
I will call her BM.
As always the topic turns to what tribe and where from.
We discover we are both from Oklahoma. He says he's Cherokee.

"Naturally," I say.

We talk.
Jim-Jack says he doesn't relate to most Indians.
He says he's never asked the government for one thing.
He says he's a self-made man.

I say Indians don't get welfare because they're Indians.
He says most Indians get Indians money. I say they don't.
He says his grandparents do. He tells me they live on the dirt around
the Arkansas River Dam, and that his people want the government
to buy, not only the dirt, but also the rocks off the top of the ground.
Jim-Jack says this embarrasses him.
He says his people are tying to gyp the government.

BM giggles and offers to buy me another drink.
I say make it a double.
BM orders dirty gin martinis.

We drink.
Jim-Jack placates me.

He says he's for supporting American Indian Museums.
He wants us to remember our past.

We argue.
Jim-Jack says he wants Indians off the government tit.
He says Indians can be proud again,
if they learn to survive without government assistance.

We order more drinks.
I offer to buy his dirty gin.
I get loud.
I want to fistfight with Jim-Jack.

I start the uproar by asking him if he's related to BIA boss Ross
        Swimmer?
I ask Jim-Jack if he's a Reagan man?

He answers no to both questions and doesn't understand I'm about
to smack him in the face with my martini glass.

Rage, rage, rage.
Indians are not a corporation.

Rage, rage, rage.
Indians will not die so we can be well thought of. So we can become part of a traveling museum exhibit at Southern Methodist University.

Rage, rage, rage.
I will castrate this man,
this cultural eunuch with my hands,
with my head, with my body.
I will emasculate him in the name of Red Rights.
In the name of Red Earth.
In the name of my grandmother who is no longer living.

Rage, rage, rage.
I will smite thine alien-enemy whose tongue is covered with hair.
I am drunk . . . .
And I realize I have seen too many Cecil B. DeMille movies.
I turn and see the image of my grandmother in the mirror.
She is standing at the bar, beside the self-made man holding a
         martini glass.
She is silent and sad. And I put the glass down.

Choctalking on Other Realities

There is only one pigeon left in Jerusalem. It could be the weather. Perhaps his more clever relatives took refuge in the cities by the Red Sea where the climate is better. Jerusalem occupies a high plateau in Israel/Palestine. In January 1992, record snows have fallen here. Outside our hotel, ice-covered oranges weigh the trees down like leaded Christmas ornaments.

I've come to Israel as an academic tourist on a university-sponsored tour. We're told that with few natural advantages and no indigenous raw materials, apart from stone, the economy of Jerusalem has always been supported from the outside. They're entirely dependent on peace. If that's true, we want to know why Jews, Muslims, and Christians in Jerusalem have adopted the stance of a "mobilized society." Perhaps it's their heritage. Each of these religious groups has always made great sacrifices to change the status quo. Recall the Jews taking Canaan and greater Israel; the Christians capturing the Roman Empire and the New World; and the Muslims seizing Arabia, Asia and Africa. The wars of heaven.

I leave the National Palace Hotel in east Jerusalem and meander down a narrow street. The pigeon comes and goes. He sails above my head. I pass a park where the benches are vacant and gray. As the afternoon light creeps behind another ragged wall of snow clouds I stop. The bird lands just beyond my reach, and I throw him the remains of my falafel sandwich. A late breakfast. We eye each other until he draws his head back as if his attention is fixed in the distance on something no one else sees. Eventually I see it too. A group of women march toward us chanting slogans in Arabic and the sky cracks open and the pigeon flies away.

They're Palestinians. Seven women. Their arms are linked together in solidarity like a chain of paper dolls. I don't understand what they are saying but I can guess. They want to change the status quo.

I follow the procession. After all this is what I've come for. To see who is doing what to whom. Like peeping toms or UN observers, we academics do very little except tell each other what we've seen. Always in dead earnest.

Soon tourists come out of the shops to see what all the ruckus is about. The women encourage us to join their protest. In a few minutes two blue and white truckloads of soldiers arrive carrying white clubs and tear gas launchers. The women stay together as long as they can until they are broken apart by the soldiers. Many of the tourists become frantic. They run into the soldiers or away from them. People scramble in all directions.

One woman breaks away from the others and runs in the direction of the American Colony Hotel. For some unexplainable reason I run after her.

Suddenly she's behind me. I know her by the sound of her feet running. I run faster across the dirt playground. If she catches me I'll never escape. I hear her panting loudly. Her weight and large frame knocks me down. I can't breath. Her blonde face blushes red as she yanks me up by my arms.

I twist out of her grasp and run toward a fence made of chicken wire. Beyond it is the WA-HE Café in Bethany, Oklahoma. Indians are inside drinking coffee and gossiping about the weather. If I make it to the WA-He they'll protect me. But she tackles me again. Hammers my head with her elbow. Sweat pours out of her body and wets my face. I gag trying not to swallow. A second white teacher comes to her aid. Together they carry me toward a small building, the kindergarten school connected to their church. They open the broom closet and shove me inside. The door slams shut.

I am still running.

THIS IS THE STORY I REALLY WANTED TO TELL

It was so hot in the kitchen of the Oklahoma City airport café that the plastic clock melted. Time oozed down the wall just like Salvador Dali imagined. The metal pieces of the flimsy clock went, "clink, clank, ting" as they hit the floor. That's because the steaks were burning, the beans were boiling, and Nina the Ukrainian, had pulled a butcher knife on Gretchen the German. There is a war going on. I am in uniform. But I race ahead of myself. This story begins in 1970.

First there are the characters.

Gretchen the German. A Catholic. The blonde cook with the white hairnet pulled down over her ears like a helmet. A Berliner, she escaped Nazi Germany during World War II to come to America and cook wiener schnitzels. That's what she tells all the customers at the airport café.

Susan B. Anthony. The black, six-foot-tall-night-cook-in-charge, Susan B. likes the blues. Speaks choicest Gullah. Cooks like snapping fingers in time. Her great-great-grandmother was a slave. Every night at the airport café she says, "Honey, don't mess with me." And I don't.

Nina. A Russian Jew from the Ukraine, she wears a white cotton uniform with socks held up by rubber bands. Nina's thumb is tattooed and causes people to stare impolitely. She says she escaped the massacre at Babi Yar. Each night she chisels perfect heads of lettuce into identical salads and weighs each portion. She is quite insane.

And me. An Oklahoma Choctaw. The waitress in the yellow uniform at the airport café. I'm a union steward for the International Brotherhood of Hotel, Motel, and Restaurant Workers of America; I'm nineteen years old and have been baptized many times. The Southern Baptists, the Nazarenes, even the Mormons got to me. Finally, I've given up being a religious consumer to become a socialist. The AFL-CIO is going to send me to college.

The Scene.

The airport café. Feeding time. The fall of 1970. Nightshift comes through the looking glass walls of the airport café. Braniff and United Airlines roar out of sight to exotic places. Somewhere a radio blasts Leon Russell's singing, " . . . *Here comes Uncle Sam again with the same old bag of beans. Local chiefs on the radio, we got some hungry mouths to feed, goin' back to Alcatraz.*"

At 6:30 p.m, one hundred Vietnam draftees drag into the Oklahoma City airport café. Afros, pork-chop sideburns, crew cuts,

Indian braids. After two years, hairless pimpled faces all look alike. Some smell bad. Some have beautiful teeth.

It's not news at the airport café that the Vietnam War is being fought disproportionately by the poor. Every Monday through Friday we serve red and yellow, black, and poor white boys their last supper as civilians. They're on their way to boot camp. They clutch their government orders and puke-belch to themselves. Their hands shake. My hands are steady. I want to tell them to run. But don't.

"No one gets hurt if they do what they're told," whispered the white teacher through the door of the broom closet. "Would you like to come out now?"

"Curious," booms a voice across the airport café's dining room. Some of the draftees look toward the kitchen, others continue eating as if they'd heard nothing.

The voice gathers strength and explodes.

"There were no survivors of Babi Yar," roars Gretchen grimly.

I rush through the kitchen door. The steaks are burning, and the beans are boiling over the fire, and Gretchen is scrutinizing Nina in front of the gas grill.

"Your story is certainly unfamiliar to me. You probably branded your own thumb so people won't accuse you. Very clever."

Nina's eyes make a circle of the kitchen. She examines her work; the stainless steel bins of freshly washed lettuce, tomatoes, radish flowers, onions, carrots, and watermelon balls. All are arranged, lined up in neat rows at her workstation. "I do what I am told," she says pushing her head against the walk-in freezer. "The sins of my occupation."

"What a wreck you are. Always building a pile of shadows," says Gretchen grabbing a slice of onion.

Nina's mouth is set in a fold of bitterness. "I know Babi Yar. It's a ravine near Kiev where the Germans murdered 35,000 Jews in September 1941. By 1943, it had become a mass grave for more than 100,000 Jews." She looks at something beyond us then screams. "I WAS THERE!"

"Yes, but what did you do?"

Nina charges Gretchen with a butcher knife in one hand, and a watermelon scoop in the other. Gretchen holds a small toaster oven in front of her like a shield. Together they dance around the room like a couple of marionettes being pulled by the fingers of God.

Eventually Susan B. Anthony interrupts the madness and Gretchen shouts, "SCHWEIG, du Neger!"

This is where I come in. I intercede like a good union steward should. Susan B. Anthony holds a hot pan of grease and is set to attack them both. The World War II survivors are screaming in languages I can't understand and pointing their weapons. They all scare the hell out of me because I'm unarmed.

1970 is a terrible year to be a teenage Indian in Oklahoma City. Vietnam is on television, nightly. World War II is still going on in the kitchen of the airport café, and I'm losing my classmates to mortar fire in Asia. Emmet Tahbone is dead. Blown away, literally. Richard Warrior is MIA, and George Billy has a shrapnel mouth.

This past week there were sit-ins at a downtown department store where blacks are still being refused services at the lunch counter. For almost ten months American Indians have occupied the abandoned prison on Alcatraz Island. The word on the streets of Oklahoma City is that we're fed up with colonialism. American Indians are finally going to change the status quo. Standing in the middle of the kitchen with my palms turned upward, a sign that I carry no weapons, I squint like a mourner who draws the curtains against the light. I feel powerless to change anything.

I look out the window and a moonbeam is crisscrossing a watery plain. It's the Pearl River with its saw grass islands and Cypress knees rising out of the water like hands in prayer to Hashtali, whose eye is the Sun. This light once cut clear across the heavens and down to the Choctaw's ancient mother mound, the Nanih Waiya in the Lower Mississippi Valley. Now it's no longer visible except on special occasions.

I see a Choctaw woman, her daughter, and their relatives. They're being attacked by a swarm of warriors from another tribe. Unfortunately bad weather has driven them into a little bayou.

They're exposed from head to foot to their enemies, the Cherokees, who've been following them for days. The Choctaw woman shows her daughter how to be brave. Several times she runs and cuts the powder horns loose from her dead relatives in order to distribute them among the living. Finally the seven warriors, and the mother and daughter, seeing that they can no longer hold their ground rush headlong upon their enemies.

A feminine voice interrupts my vision. *"No one gets hurt if they do what they're told."* I shake my head trying to drive it out of me. *"We fly daily non-stop flights to locations across America, Europe, and Asia,"* continues the recorded message on the airport's loudspeaker.

I turn back to my co-workers who are drowning in a pool of tears. "No one will get hurt if we do what we're supposed to do," I say meekly. For a moment no one moves. Then they begin struggling with their kitchen utensils. Suddenly Nina is composed, Gretchen too, both of them square their shoulders the way soldiers do when called to attention. They promise it will never happen again, but no one believes them.

At midnight the lines on my face have melted like the clock in Salvador Dali's painting. I resemble a sad clown. When Susan B. Anthony and I walk outside to share a smoke we eye one other wearily.

"What happened?" I ask quietly.

"God knows," she says lighting a cigarette.

Together we watch as the lights of a crayon-colored Braniff jet leave a trail of stale dead air, and I think I'll buy a mask and become someone else. The AFL-CIO can't save me now.

Choctalking On Other Realities

I did become someone else. A mother, a teacher, a writer, a wife. When the opportunity came to visit Israel in 1992, I signed up for the two-week trip at the behest of my husband, a geographer and co-leader of the study tour. We are going to Jerusalem to learn about the affects of the Intifada on the region and its peoples. At first, I was hesitant. The very word Jerusalem connotes religion. Three of them: Judaism, Christianity, Islam, birthed in that order. They all look the same to me. They share one God known as Yahweh, Allah, or Jesus. They honor the same prophets. They share many of the same books. Their holidays center around religious and cultural victories over each other. Kind of like Americans celebrating Thanksgiving. Holidays are the masks of conquerors.

But wouldn't you know it. On my first day in Jerusalem I met a Jewish woman who said her great-grandmother was a Cherokee.

She tells me it is a long story — how one side of her family immigrated to America, then re-immigrated to Israel after 1948. I stand motionless and look at the woman across the glass counter of her gift shop. Listen skeptically to the ragged tenderness of her story. The weary but elusive Indian ancestry, the fawning desire to be related to me, at least my Indianness, is something I've experienced before.

I study the shopkeeper's face. We are remarkably alike. Black eyes. Dark hair. About the same age. As the shadows of Jerusalem invade her shop windows I grow nostalgic. The city looms under a delicious haze of smoke from the outdoor falafel stands, and I want to take this woman away with me. To cross time and the ocean together. To place her in our past, to put myself in her beginning, and intertwine our threads of history —for we are nothing without our relationships. That's Choctaw.

I begin my story in the middle "Choctaws are not originally from Oklahoma. We are immigrants too."

The woman whose ancestor was a Cherokee nods her head as if she understands, and I continue.

"Our ancient homelands are in the Southeastern part of the United States where we were created in the spectacular silken flatness of the delta lands. The earth opened her body and beckoned us to join her above ground so our ancestors tunneled up through her navel into tinges of moist red men and women. We collected our chins, knees, breasts, and sure-footed determination — long before Moses parted the Red Sea, and the God with three heads was born in the Middle East.

"Choctaws were the second largest allied group of peoples in the south east. Our population centers were clustered like wheels around three major rivers: to the east the Tombigbee River; to the west the Pearl River; and in the South the Chickasawhay River. We made trading relationships with other tribes in our regions whenever possible."

She interrupts my story, asks me if I will come to her house for an evening meal. She talks on. Says that she went to school in New York City, and that she misses the company of Americans. Her own mother is dead, since she was a child. All she has left is her father, the one who owns the shop. She looks at me. "You promise to tell me more of your history?"

"What I can."

Her home is west of Jerusalem. Opposite the old city where everyone walks instead of rides. There are great American-style streets full of Mercedes, Peugeots and Perrier bottles. Her place is elegant, an estate on a hill. There's a dark studio with a mahogany desk, Navajo rugs, and an enormous basket made from the skeleton of a Saguaro tree sits near the stone fireplace. She builds a fire against the cold and opens the shutters to let in the city. She says she doesn't feel anything in particular toward the Arabs, no hate, and no repulsion either. I asked her what about the Choctaws? She smiles, not knowing what I mean. She says she is where she has to be. Placed here. Of course she feels a tinge of fear. It's as if this is not only what she expects, but what must happen to her.

She says she pays closest attention to the noise of the city. That the city shouts what is going to happen. The explosions, the bullets, the prayers, the celebratory demonstrations, they're all part of it she says, like messages from God.

She begins telling me some rigmarole about how Jerusalem meets the needs of all its people. Throughout its four-thousand-year history she says the city was meant to be a place of unity. Her father believes that now the Intifada is over there can be peace between the Arabs and Jews.

Behind her a shadow walks into the room. I see the image of a woman in darned socks. I think I recognize her face, but I can't quite make it out, so speak up without waiting for a polite pause in our conversation.

"Then why, every day, do Jews and Arabs try and kill one another?"

"Why did Indians sell Manhattan to the Christians?"

Night comes through the shutters. The din of the streets below grows louder. It's more penetrating than the livid red streetlamps.

We look at each other. Our expressions are suddenly changed. We realize we're on the side of societies that have reduced us to grief.

All the same she rushes to tell me the story of her great-grandfather, a shoemaker, an outcast in North Carolina just like her great-grandmother, the Cherokee. "He was in exile, she was conquered. They fell in love because they had this in common. After World War II my grandfather, the one who was half-Jewish-half-Cherokee, made a pilgrimage to the Holy Land. He never returned to America."

"Indians are not conquered!"

"But your nerve is gone," she says, sadly. "I was a student at New York City University when the Indians surrendered Alcatraz Island in June 1971. We would have never given up."

There is a long silence.

"Who is we?" I ask.

"I've provoked you," she says. "Now I give you the chance to give me a piece of your mind."

There was a trace of something odd in her remark, so I began with a metaphor. "Once a very ancient god came back from everywhere. Arriving at a banquet in his honor with a bundle of keys, he announced that it was closing time, and toilets around the world exploded."

We laugh. It breaks the tension.

"It's from the good book. The missing pages."

"And then what happened?" she asks. "You promised to tell me your history."

"After the war ended between the British and the French in 1763 Indians in the Southeast couldn't make the foreigners do anything. Soldiers went AWOL and married into our tribes. No one wanted to live in Paris or London anymore. That's why so many Choctaws, Creeks, Chickasaws and Cherokees have British and French last names.

"In 1830, after the Treaty of Dancing Rabbit Creek was signed, the Choctaw are the first to be removed from our ancient homelands. Many walked all the way with very little to eat or drink. The road to the Promised Land was terrible. Dead horses and their dead riders littered the way. Dead women lay in the road with babies dried to their breasts, tranquil as if napping. A sacred compost for scavengers."

She stokes the fire to keep it from dying, and I know the more revolting the details, the less she believes me. Finally she says. "You are exaggerating."

"Perhaps. But four thousand Choctaws died immigrating to Oklahoma."

"It is late," she says, ignoring my facts. "Time I returned you to your hotel. I'm sure your husband is waiting for you."

"But you said you wanted to know about my history?"

She gives me a fishy look but agrees. "Very well."

"It's no accident that there are sixty-six Indian Nations headquartered in Oklahoma. Oklahoma or Indian Territory was a forerunner of Israel. Choctaws were the first to be removed there, other Indian tribes from around country soon followed. We were supposed to live together in peace. Form relationships. It wasn't easy, but for the most part we did it because we do not idealize war. However throughout the nineteenth century more and more whites moved into Indian Territory. Followed by missionaries and lawyers who began converting us, or swindling us."

"Then on April 22, 1889 the American government opened the unassigned lands to the whites. When the trumpet sounded, the

Run of 1889 began. It was estimated that twenty thousand immigrants were waiting at the border to stake their claims. Today the Run of 1889 is an annual celebration in Oklahoma. Like a holiday."

"I thought you were going to tell me *your* story."

"I'm coming to it," I answer, pausing to clear my throat. "There was no color in the broom closet. Light edged around the door. There may have been other teachers outside the closet, but I only knew of her by the smell of her sweat.

"The church had started a kindergarten program. She was a missionary. That morning the preacher said we were lucky to have a missionary lead us in a song. "*Red and yellow, black and white we are separate in his sight, Jesus loves the little children of the world.*" Then I sang it several times by myself. I was only repeating what I thought I heard. The words had no meaning for me, I was five years old. When she marched toward me shaking her fist, with that mouth of angry nails I panicked and ran outside across the playground and toward a café.

"Down, down, down, the fall crushes me, and I'm mucking around in the dirt. She oozed through my pores that hot afternoon in Bethany Oklahoma, and there she has remained whispering inside my head."

I stare at my host. "It isn't that we lost our nerve. Sometimes we're just overwhelmed."

After I finish my story, a strange quiet grips the Jewish woman whose ancestor was a Cherokee. Her face becomes attentive, as if listening to something that penetrated her soul.

When she drops me off at the National Palace hotel, I watch her drive away. All I can think of is that she's right, that Jerusalem, "the city of peace" is what is meant to happen to her.

The next day I rejoin our study tour and we meet some Palestinian women from the Gaza Strip. In 1992 the Gaza Strip is still one of the Occupied Territories of Israel. The Palestinian women tell us their stories through an interpreter. One woman says that the government prohibits them from displaying the colors of the Palestinian flag, which are green, red, black and white. She says her husband has been arrested for having a picture of a watermelon on his desk. Many others show us empty tear-gas canisters that have been shot into their homes by the soldiers. They are plainly marked, "MADE IN USA."

To show concern for the Palestinians some members of our study tour present the women with duffel bags full of used clothes and high heel shoes marked MADE IN USA. I didn't bring any used clothes, so I ask the Christian coordinator from the Council of Middle East Churches if I could give the Palestinian women money instead of used clothes.

"No," she replies. "They'll just come to expect it from us."

The next day when the study tour leaves for a two-day visit for Nazareth, I stay behind at our hotel. I've had enough. I want to be alone, walk the streets of the old city, and eat in the small cafés.

Throughout the day prayers are broadcast over loudspeakers. For Muslims, the first prayer of the day begins at the moment the rays of the sun begin to appear on the horizon. The last prayer in the evening ends at sunset. Devout Jews pray three times a day; devout Muslims pray five times daily. When I hear a man singing the prayers on a mosque's loud speaker system I am sure he is praying to the Sun, just like Choctaws once prayed to Hashtali.

"The prayers are to Allah, not the Sun," says a vendor outside the Al-Aqsa Mosque in Jerusalem.

"It looks like you are praying to the Sun, especially with your palms turned up toward the sky. The Egyptians once worshipped the sun God, RA. Since the Hebrews and the Egyptians once lived together, maybe your religions rubbed off on each other. Everyone in this country says "Yis-RA-el" for Israel. Maybe there's a relationship?

He waved me away. "No, no, no, you have been misinformed! There is no God, but the God of us all."

I Am Still Running

Palestinian men from around the community race past me toward the soldiers and meet them head-on. The protest explodes into a riot. Mothers, daughters, and grandmothers from inside the shops join the women in the streets. The soldiers begin dragging people inside the blue and white paddy wagons, one or two at a time, amidst weeping and bleeding fists.

I run toward the leader crumpled against the stonewall. Suddenly I recognize her. It's Nina from the airport café. I can't believe it, but it's really Nina. She's dressed in her white cotton uniform, her shabby socks still held up with rubber bands. A soldier reaches her before me.

"Don't hurt her, it's Nina. Can't you see? She's a survivor of Babi Yar."

Suddenly I'm on the ground. I cannot breath. Someone rifles through my purse and pulls out my American passport. He yanks me up by my arms and tells me in English to go home.

"No one gets hurt if they do what they're told."

"No, it's a lie. RUN!" I scream so loud that I frighten the voice out of my head.

Nina gets up and tries to jump the stone fence, but the soldier bashes her in the legs with a club. She falls down and he carries her to the paddy wagon and shoves her inside.

I am back to the dubious place where memory distorts fragments of an indivisible experience and we meet a different self. It wasn't Nina the soldier carried into the government vehicle. She died talking to God that terrible night in the airport café. She collapsed on the floor of the kitchen, not long after the fight with Gretchen, asking God why she had to die, why now that she'd regained her courage. "Very well," was all she whispered.

Standing in the middle of the street in east Jerusalem, I watch the determined faces of the Palestinian women and weep for Nina. I still believe she is with the Palestinian protesters, just as I believe she was at Babi Yar.

An Arab member of the Knesset, the Israeli parliament, finally arrives in a government car and calls for calm. He holds both hands out to the soldiers, a sign that he carries no weapons.

The pigeon returns and lands next to me, as if surveying the waste. The Knesset member sees us, stops, then walks on with his palms facing toward the sun. I will believe the rest of my life that this is what he prayed for.

"Save her. She is the Jewish women shot to death by the Germans at Babi Yar.

"Save her. She is the Palestinian women shot to death by the Jews at Deir Yassin.

"Save her. She is the Vietnamese women shot to death by the Americans at Mi Lai.

"Save her. She is the Mayan women shot to death by the Mexicans in Chiapas."

"Save her. She is the Black women shot to death by the Ku Klux Klan in Alabama."

"Save her. She is The People, our grandmothers, our mothers, our sisters, our ancestors, ourselves.

"Save us."

Cannibalism

A Duck's Tune

*Ya kut unta pishno ma**
Ya kut unta pishno ma
Ya kut unta pishno ma
Ya kut unta pishno ma

So I moved to this place,
Iowa City, Ioway
Where green-headed mallards
walk the streets day and night,
and defecate on sidewalks.
Greasy meat bags in wetsuits,
disguise themselves as pets
and are as free as birds.
Maybe Indians should have thought of that?

Ya kut unta pishno ma
Ya kut unta pishno ma
Ya kut unta pishno ma
Ya kut unta pishno ma

Maybe you would have
left us alone,
if we put on rubber bills,
and rubber feet,
Quacked instead of complained,
Swam instead of danced
waddled away when you did
what you did . . .

Ya kut unta pishno ma
Ya kut unta pishno ma
Ya kut unta pishno ma
Ya kut unta pishno ma

* This is a dance refrain for a song. The phrase is to be performed. Ya kut unta
pishno ma means *"We were doing this." Dancing.*

So I moved to the place
The "Jewel of the Midwest"
Where ghosts of ourselves
Dance the sulphur trails.

Fumes emerge continuous
from the mouths of
Three-faced Deities who preach,
"We absolve joy through suffering."

Ya kut unta pishno ma
Ya kut unta pishno ma
Ya kut unta pishno ma
Ya kut unta pishno ma

So I moved to this place where
in 1992, up washed Columbus again
like a pointy-chinned Son of Cannibals.
His spin doctors rewrite his successes
"After 500 years and 25 million dead,
One out of 100 American Indians commit suicide
One out of 10 American Indians are alcoholics
49 years is the average lifespan of American Indians."

Each minute burns
the useful and useless alike
Sing Hallelujah
Praise the Lord

Ya kut unta pishno ma
Ya kut unta pishno ma
Ya kut unta pishno ma
Ya kut unta pishno ma

And when you foreigners
build your off-world colonies
and relocate in outer space
This is what we will do
We will dance,
We will dance,
We will dance
to a duck's tune.

Ya kut unta pishno ma
Ya kut unta pishno ma
Ya kut unta pishno ma
Ya kut unta pishno ma

A Carbon Isotopic Perspective on Dietary Variation in Late Prehistoric Times: Or, Friends I have Loved and Ingested

In August 1989, the World Archaeological Congress held its First Inter-Congress in Vermillion, South Dakota. The Inter-Congress conducted its meetings in association with the World Council of Indigenous Peoples, the International Indian Treaty Council, and American Indians Against Desecration. The topic of the Inter-congress was archaeology, and the ethical treatment of the indigenous dead. The so-called "Reburial issue." It was the first worldwide meeting between anthropologists, archaeologists, American Indian activists, and indigenous peoples to discuss — who owns whom. Who will consume whom?

EYE OF THE STORM

The Indian faction we formed in Vermillion
The World's Indigenous Congress,
The WIC,
Lit a fire.
The circle we formed
in the hallway
of the building
where the Western World gathered to discuss
the Ethical Treatment For the Indigenous Dead
had held strong.
The Greeks, The Brits, The Italians, and the Germans
Agreed.
There will be no more digging
without indigenous consent.

So on this tenth day of the tenth of the month
WIC members talked of Indian rodeos,
of PowWows.
Of making our own clothes from
the skin and bones of animals.
Of Prayers.
We joked of riding the Dakota horse to success.
Earlier that week

alone in my room
I had called on Hawk Woman, the Grandmother
who circles above us to help me.
I told her I didn't want to end up
on someone's specimen table
or in a slide show that the pale Dr. Otto
had prepared for his American classes.

While searching my face
like some thirsty mosquito
looking for an open vein
Dr. Otto, a panelist at the conference
had said that Indian skulls
are more aesthetically pleasing than his own.
Looking into his face I realized
I couldn't argue with him.

WHO OWNS THE PAST?
WHO OWNS THE FUTURE?
WHO OWNS GRANDMOTHER?

But on that last day,
the Indians
did not speak of our dead.
We did not speak of
reburial,
or our ancestors
trapped under glass
displayed in museums
like zoo animals behinds bars.
On this morning we are laughing
in the hall.
Lisa is on the telephone
giving her secretary a tongue lashing
for booking her flight incorrectly.
Joe sits on the couch
smoking hand rolled cigarettes.
His black, waist length hair hangs loosely around his shoulders.
Joe is converting Dr. Faust.
On this morning Dr. Faust looks pensive,
filled with questions;
troubled by things he does not understand.

A Carbon Isotopic Perspective on Dietary Variation In Late Prehistoric Times: Or, Friends I have loved and analyzed

Joe takes short drags from his tobacco.
He is on the attack. Joe's soft voice lowers to
a whisper as he pulls Dr. Faust
closer for the killing embrace.
What the good doctor cannot know is that
Like God,—what we love, we also devour. . . ingest. . . . become.
"And I am in you, and you are in me.
wrote the man who wooed mankind. "

I look away from the two men on the couch.
When I look back Dr. Faust is gone.

The Indians at the conference in Vermillion
continue laughing
We call attention to ourselves
We are laughing about nothing visible
and as I've noted many times,
When you laugh — of nothing —
sooner or later
someone gets nervous.

EVERYBODY NEEDS SOME BODY SOMETIME!
WE ARE NOT SINNERS, SAVAGES OR CRIMINALS
WE DO NOT NEED CLERGYMEN, ANTHROPOLOGISTS
OR POLICE . . . J. T. PATTON 1938

On this last day I will not leave you behind.
Imagine my surprise, archaeologists, anthropologists, and
     Indian Activists
do not mix well when stirred.
We are on opposites sides of the graveyard,
After all, who am I to pick on an archaeologist?
"Sooner or later one of them will come for you, anyway!"
That's what Grandmother shouted, as she drove away in her
18-wheeler. She is usually right.

Finders Keepers: Aboriginal Responses to European Colonization

Almost three hundred years ago
Mississippi Choctaw women took
Frenchmen into their beds
into their *iksas*,
into their hearts
for their blood.
The men called this ritual
the sweet medicine of immortality.

Bread is the human body
Bread confers immortality.
When my story is finished,
You will offer yourself again to me like bread.
Unafraid.
And I will take you.
My God you are brave.
Have you forgotten what Grandmother said?

That the women of my family
are like the plants
we call *bashuchak*.
Everlastings

ARCHAEOLOGY AND THE VANISHING INDIAN

This is a story of reconciliations.
Of friends we love and ingest.
And I am in you and you are in me.
Isn't that what your God said, too?
Driving down the road
Grandmother passes us again in her 18-wheeler
Waving a feathered wing out the window.
She squeals, "No guts No glory."

The List We Make

FIRST NOTE:

America is 82 percent Christian. 60 percent of the population believes the Bible is historical fact. The President of the United States has endorsed Jesus as his favorite philosopher.

SECOND NOTE

From today's perspective, cannibalism among early Indians appears to have had a greater stringency than was actually the case. The inclination of history to list these incidents creates the impression that opposing groups simply ate each other as a way of ending conflict. We did not have the aim of discovering cannibalism, but discovering what was in us. . . . [1]

THIRD NOTE:

As Catherine Albanese has shown, Anglo-American literature transformed Davy Crockett from a frontier settler and soldier into a violent superhero communing with the overwhelming spirit of the wilderness by killing and eating bears and Creek Indians. [2]

---

[1] From an email conversation between myself and University of California, Riverside Professor Geoff Cohen, concerning his class "The Iconography of Cannibal in Early American Literature." 2004.

[2] From an email conversation between myself and University of California, Riverside Professor Joel Martin concerning Davy Crockett and his exploits with Indians. 2004.

FOURTH NOTE:

Luis and Salvadore, the two Miwok guides for the 1846 Donner
Party were the first to be shot and eaten as food. For many American
Indians, Luis and Salvadore represent us all:

William Foster had become deranged, and it is understandable why,
knowing what he endured. He was terrified he would die from
starvation, and Foster planned on murdering the Indians for food.
Eddy, a friend told Luis and Salvadore, who promptly ran away. The
party followed the tracks of Luis and Salvadore. It was easy. The feet
of the Indians had become so raw from exposure all their toes had
fallen off, marking their trail with blood. Foster figured if the
Indians didn't lead them to safety, they could at least find their
corpses to use as food.

By January 9th or 10th, the Indians had suffered terrible exposure
to the cold, and had survived on practically nothing to eat, with no
fire. They couldn't last like that. They gave out near a small creek,
and it was here the Forlorn Hope came upon them. Despite
argument from some and the Indians look of terror, Foster shot the
two Indians with his rifle. Though they would not have lived long,
the act was horrifying. [3]

---

3 From the website: The Donner Party by Daniel Lewis.
   http://railboy.tripod.com/donner/

PART 2

The waiting road
arrives
this time San Francisco
moves along the abyss
in a black car filled with dawn and
men's underwear.

Again,
a membrane binds us
and I crave all you offer
your hands,
your poets' wrists that bleed
on the page
your penis of words
that penetrates my vagina
like a wet weapon.

We drape our bodies with new surroundings,
But like moveable sets on a theater stage
we fear hammer and nails,
hunger,
death,
longing,
and consumption.

We café
trying to remember who we are,
for each other, I mean.
At Dollys, wide omelets,
Big cups of brown Espresso unearth
old hungers, centuries old,
beckon.
"Yes," curves us together

and we breathe in the same thin air
We breathe in each other
and forget all that has happened.

On the road made flesh
they separate us
from our fingers and toes
separate us from our bones.
At first, we are swallowed whole
like the wafers of God
down the gullets of hungry Christians.
Everything we did, everything we didn't do
is digested in their dreams
Now they know us better than we knew ourselves

On the lam (again) we head north to the casinos
becoming what we fear: Consumers of goods and services.
We give twenty dollars to a stranger
to teach us how
to attach chains so
we can slip past Donner Pass
where banquet chairs pose
still as icicles
patiently awaiting our return.

We race toward the Biltmore Motel
Our music is hard sevens
We lunch in the high Sierras and
You teach me to gamble.
We crash a writer's conference
A bad poet reads an 'ode to appetite'
But this time we will not be dinner.

PART 3

Seven thousand feet up
though Lake Tahoe stalks us
we practice our escape by devouring a
repugnant pig like our killers once devoured us.
At the All-American Café
You in grey to my conventional black,
we dine on goose liver,
pineapple, and curried ice cream
Where are Luis and Salvadore now?
Who the hell cares! We're following
a treasure map of flesh and blood,
the ghost camouflage of exotic appetites
that came for Luis and Salvadore,
has infected us all
And,
what of this steamy you and I?
This steam,
This you and I?
Imprisoned by a hoary's God's ravenous hunger
we have not shadow's gaze
Nor eyes and ears.
No shadowy past.
Nothing, but here and now
made manifest within a complexion of stars
Our bodies
Geometry now
Conjoined in the heavens
On earth as
Luis y Salvadore
Conjoined in blood,
And oddly enough
Love.

My Name Is Noble Savage

I was built for iconography
Break my hymen
I bleed and reproduce
Children you sketch
and photograph,
Catalogue,
But soon abandon.

How many wounds do you hope I carry?

My name is Noble Savage
Wanna rent me for a day?
A week?
A year?
By the hour?
I'm the story you finger-fucked
the evidence under your fingernail
Can you feel me coming for you?

My name is Noble Savage
You killed me
In order to bring me back to life
As your pet, a mascot
A man.
Since I'm your invention
Everything I say comes true.

My name is Noble Savage
America's redeemer.
Tonight,
alone with my murderer,
iconographer
May your God have
Mercy on your soul.

Disney's Pocahontas Longs for Noble Savage

When you find me,
I'll be your pool of DNA
A carrier of a million fiery red eggs
where you may plant
longing that I will trade my life for
each and every time you enter me.

I will fuck 47
Make love to thousands more
Birth a nation of sons and daughters.

They will all be a substitute for you,

Noble Savage Sees A Therapist

NOBLE SAVAGE: She's too intense for me.
                  And I feel nothing. No emotion.
                  In fact, I'm off all females
                  —even lost my lust for
                  attacking white chicks.

(Pause.)

THERAPIST: (He writes furiously on a yellow pad, but says
                  nothing.)

NOBLE SAVAGE: People expect me to be strong,
                  Wise,
                  Stoic,
                  Without guilt.
                  A man capable of a few symbolic acts.
                  Ugh—is that what I'm supposed to say?

THERAPIST: (He continues writing.)

NOBLE SAVAGE: I don't feel like
                  Maiming,
                  Scalping,
                  Burning wagon trains.
                  I'm developing hemorrhoids
                  from riding bareback.
                  It's an impossible role.
                  The truth is I'm conflicted.
                  I don't know who I am.
                  What should I do, Doc?

THERAPIST: I'm afraid we've run out of time. Let's take
                  this up during our next visit.

The Indian Sports Mascot Meets Noble Savage

INDIAN MASCOT: I think of us always as a couple.

NOBLE SAVAGE: Have we ever been together? Are we ever going to be?

INDIAN MASCOT: But here we are. You with a bow and arrow. Me in a headdress.

NOBLE SAVAGE: We've never been together.

INDIAN MASCOT: Do you ever dream of us?

NOBLE SAVAGE: No.

INDIAN MASCOT: I do. And when I do, you look just like me.

Noble Savage Confronts Indian Mascot

NOBLE SAVAGE: What are you doing in my closet?

INDIAN MASCOT: Sugar, can I wear your loin cloth to the big
game tonight?

NOBLE SAVAGE: No, and don't call me sugar.

INDIAN MASCOT: C'mon. Besides, you've outgrown it.

NOBLE SAVAGE: No I haven't. Take off those feathers.

INDIAN MASCOT: You said you liked my ostrich boa.

NOBLE SAVAGE: Only that one time. I wish you'd forget it.

INDIAN MASCOT: I will never forget it.

NOBLE SAVAGE: I don't feel the same about you.

INDIAN MASCOT: Don't pull that colonizer shit with me, baby.
First you say you love me, then you say you don't. I'm not
your toy boy. Listen, I'm the better half of you six days of
the week, and twice on Sunday. (He screams and goes a
little crazy.) And don't you forget it!

(Long Pause)

NOBLE SAVAGE: (shrugs) Sorry.

Noble Savage Contemplates His Fate

Dear Diary;
I can't fall in love with anyone.
I'm here to make all men believe
They're just like me.

Indian Mascot Joins The Village People

At last,
I'm in step with Hollywood,
No longer a transitory subaltern
On center stage
I surpass Fred Astaire,
Michael Jackson,
his sister,
and,
(You can't touch this)
Beatboxer Alien Dee.

I'm masculine prowess
a male dancer in beads and skins,
See the stadium crowd
how they jump to their feet in a
Reverent,
Religious,
Fervent,
Fit.
"YMCA, YMCA, YMCA, YMCA"
an old chant—
Young Men's Christian Association
Young Men's Christian Association
Young Men's Christian Association
Young Men's Christian Association.

Yeah, some decades are more ironic than others.

Indian Mascot Encounters Prejudice
(from real Indians)

My own people hate me.
When the Red woman and her child see me,
They weep.
And I weep, too.
"He's white," the Indians, cry. "He's a bestial impersonator."
I try to humor them with my beautiful smile,
My half-time fancy footwork,
but they throw rotten apples,
At moi.
"You're a fiction." They shout.
"A character, that much is certain." I reply.
"An invention?" They chant.
"No more than you!"
"A failure?" They charge.
"Not a chance. I have fans."
And the show must go on.

American Indians Attempt to Assassinate
Indian Mascot

Now,
only the whites protect me.
Indians scream, "Monster."
"He inspires disgust," they cry.
They're words sting like bullets.
Where is my Noble Savage when I need him?
He always defends the weak.

In defiance, I mock my detractors,
"Not butch enough for you, *eh?*"
I pull out all the stops.
Listen,
"I fought beside Red Shoes against the British in 1720."
"I fought with Little Turtle at the 1794 Battle of Fallen Timbers."
"I fought at Horseshoe Bend in the 1814 Red Stick War."
"And, I *KILLED* Custer at the Battle of Little Big Horn."

An Indian boy will not stand for my blasphemy.
He draws his revolver from a backpack,
Aims,
Fires,
Dead on,
Straight.
At the last possible moment my beloved
rides to the rescue on a white horse,
and
we take the bullet simultaneously.
Mortally wounded,
We sigh together.

Ah, my love.

What happened to Indian Mascot and Noble Savage—
　　After the shooting?

Nothing.
They were never real.
This is Hollywood.

The Way We Were—Indian Mascot Laments
His Lost Love, Anyway

Finally,
You quit your job
Find work with
The Gendamerie royale
du Canada,
The Royal Canadian Mounted Police,
Marry an astronaut
Father and Mother
57 wooden Indians.

I move to Bilbao
Fall for a Basque politician
who adores a
proud symbol
such as myself

But sadly,
there is only you for me.
Your tender hands on my hips
Your eyes, deep as an abyss,
Your savage thighs.

Remember our first trip to Quebec City
where we found ourselves
in the little shop of *Figurines Rouges*?
And how we escaped the academics
by driving fast in a red convertible
with the top down.
In the snow.

Our very first fight?
Our last?

Alone at the Bullfights
A frayed avatar,
I prostitute myself
for a guitar band,
for the money.
And afterwards
I inhale too much red wine,
too much fried squid ink
too many pintxos.

In my dreams,
I wander the riverwalk
next to The Guggenheim
hoping to spot
images of the two of us
in the museum
where at last
we may rest side-by-side
Protected sacred objects
in a dim light.
Dark figures
rising
as only
Memory.

Ballad of Red Sorrow

A red cardinal
knocks at my window
beating himself senseless
against the glass pane

It's illusion
that draws him,
not my seed,
nor swollen larva

A believer,
he fights an invisible enemy
who may well devour everything
Don't give up, I whisper

The cardinal's drumbeat thuds on
as the glass smears with fresh blood
I open the window and
join the red warrior in battle

Grabbing his flopping wings
I close my fingers
and squeeze.
You win, I whisper

Freedom for us all

Still Code Talking

Choctaw Chief Cobb to Captain J.J. McRea,
Choctaw Council 1843:

Brother: when you were young, we were strong: we fought by your side, but our arms are now broken. You have grown large. My people have become small.

Brother: My voice is weak; you can scarcely hear me; it is not the shout of a warrior, but the wail of an infant. I have lost it in mourning over the misfortunes of my people. There are their graves, and in those aged pines you hear the ghosts of the departed. —their ashes are here and we have been left to protect them. Our warriors are nearly all gone to the far country west; but here are our dead. Shall we go too, and give their bones to the wolves?

Brother: Our hearts are full. Twelve winters ago our chiefs sold our country. Every warrior that you see here was opposed to the treaty. If the dead could have counted, it would never have been made, but alas," though they stood around, they could not be seen or heard. Their tears came in raindrops, and their voices in the wailing wind, but the pale faces knew it not, and our land was taken away.

. . . When you took our country, you promised us land. There is your promise in the book. Twelve times have the trees dropped their leaves and yet, we have received no land. Our houses have been taken from us. The white man's plough turns up the bones of our fathers. We dare not kindle our fires; and yet you said we might remain and you would give us land. [1]

Lemme see if I can translate:

You fucked us and we ain't never gonna forget it. Not now, not in ten thousand years, not ever.

[1] Niles Register LXIV 1843, 131–132.

Choctaw Code Talking

The Lie

For Joe Craig—2004

After September 11, 2001 President George W. Bush told Americans to go shopping—if it would make us feel better. So I headed first to Jordan. From there I decided to shop in the Souk in Syria into the homelands of Abraham, and St. Paul.

"Have you now, or have you ever been a practitioner of American Indian religion," asks the Syrian bureaucrat at the VISA window in Amman, Jordan. The woman speaking is in charge of granting me a one-day permit into the city of Damascus to shop in the world's oldest, continuously-operated Souk. I have written on my application that the real reason I've come to Syria is to visit the Nunnery where St. Paul, the Apostle stayed. The Syrian woman eyes me suspiciously. She's jealous of my turquoise jewelry, I know it.

"No, "I answer in Arabic. "But I do Choctaw ceremonies, and every year during Passover I watch *The Ten Commandants* on television (in my underwear) and cry. They say Moses hurled his own artwork into the desert."

I hope my dialogic imagination subverts her line of questioning— and that my Arabic, though lame, is understandable. But instead she replies in English:

"What has Charlton Heston to do with Choctaws? Are Choctaws Jews or American Indians?"

"We're American Indians." I answer in English.

"Have you now, or have you ever been intelligent," asks the Syrian matter-of-factly. "After all, American Indians do not have souls. She leans forward conspiratorially. I've seen *The Searchers* on television."

"But . . ."

"You are not people of 'The Book,'" she says. "The Jews, the Christians, the Muslims — we are all people of the book. But you are not. You have no book. Even your own President believes you are primitive and unworthy," she says, stamping my papers "REFUSED" in red ink.

"But. . . ."

She closes the VISA window.

I walk back across the Syrian guard post and into the Kingdom of Jordan. Perhaps Moses had lied and couldn't cross the border for the same reason.

Post-Mortem

The things we do in our sleep
Father's Day 1977
You drive a Jeep Cherokee into my dreams and park,
just like a cliché.
I hold the Mickey Mouse tie I once bought for you,
but boxed up instead of mailing.
We cry—

On the day you die in 1997, my mother will telephone.
I am teaching school in Northfield, Minnesota, but recollect
nothing more, except her call.
It's odd, the things we claim in moments when our lips are
        sealed.
A lost tie.
The father I didn't know
but feel like muscle and sinew

Now in our sleep we
lash memory to membrane
grafting echoes into harmony.
And we smile—

Posthumously.

Bird Woman Returns

You broke my wings with your shaft
A single arrow was all it took
All I had to go on was the scent
of brain-tanned leather,
the feel of soft leggings
So I hunted.

Even as I picked the bones of other lovers
shoving their bodies down my gullet
(I loved the noise they made in my nib)
I desired your sweat and blood
Above all others
Above their breaking bones.

No one should be that hungry

Across stars and fading comets
We slip past each other
You in Syria,
searching for clues of the Bird Woman,
The one you pulled apart,
but remembered like poetry.

And me, preening my black feathers,
flashing your picture around like the FBI.
After three hundred years,
I smell revenge in your hands,
And my menstrual blood that
 Turns bird
into woman.

— Every so often, it works like that.
Now I won't lose you for
the God of Allah, his mother, or
an Indian-head nickel

Horse Dreams

Falling asleep,
you are almost here
I inhale and push up
against your body
then mount your white horse of a back
and together we fly away
Dreaming

I kiss the words you wrote
As you paw the sky
I taste sticky lustful sweat
on your tongue
that your mouth stole from me
while we were dreaming

Kick Boxing

Indian women are mean
We make a fist
before a kiss
kick box before
opening our legs,
shout go away man,
I have no time for erotic distractions
Can't you see I am birthing a nation, our tribe, our people.

Indian men who are patient as seeds
dodge and weave and
pretend to be Muhammad Ali
even before there was Muhammad Ali, or boxing.
They taunt us with quick gibes,
Come back here woman — hit me again!
I can take your blows of little thunder
You are good practice for warriors-in-training

Hearing this,
Indian women, even the meanest of us
lie down and offer our tender weapons
In defeat
Indian men,
who knew this was coming all along
sigh,
and prepare to swallow fire.

Indians Never Say Good-bye

There she was standing over me. She inched her face close to my face. She put her hands on my face. I remembered her immediately, but did not speak. My eyes blurred. They were hot and heavy. It hurt to look at Ain't Sally. It hurt to see.

I closed my eyes. I felt her cool touch. She chanted. "You will be well. You will not die. *Chim achukma taha che.* You will be well. *Chi pesa taha che.*"

She sang to me. Then I heard her leave.

A woman whose bed was surrounded by white partitions, moaned again. This was not a new sound. It was a constant. Her breath whistled irregularly. There was no escaping the whistle. The whistling sounds were everywhere in the white room. Then they stopped.

Another woman in another bed called out. No answer. She pushed the bell. Women wearing white dresses came into the room. They pushed the partitions back. They said the whistling woman was dead. I went back to sleep. Before the hospital. Before rheumatic fever. Before the dead woman. I had met Ain't Sally. I was seven years old.

Ain't Sally was an ancient Indian relative who lived in Hayrick, outside of Dublin. A place of the Snakes. A place of memory.

Once a base camp for nomadic tribes following buffalo, once a county seat, Hayrick, Texas took its name from a solitary mountain standing in the breadth of open grasslands. Only a state government road sign remains, marking the place of Hayrick. Marking the sign of the Snakes.

The only time we visited Ain't Sally, I rode in the back seat of our green 1950 Chevrolet, and listened to my Indian grandmother tell stories about our family. Chapters went like this:

—Life in a Dugout.
—Making Lye Soap.

—How Grandfather got VD.

I don't remember much of the drive to Hayrick. We drove the rural roads of West Texas. There were two lanes of dust and dirt, stagnant, green-belted river beds and one-lane bridges.

When we arrived at Ain't Sally's the old woman ambled out of a rusted screen door of a paintless wooden house. Breasts sagging, her thin body lacking in strength seemed unable to support her weight. She wore a sleeveless dress that revealed naked brown skin, skin that was no more than a sheath for aging bones. Hairless underarms.

She fed us saltine crackers and cold squirrel dumplings. She asked me questions. She asked me about my secrets. I don't remember having any to tell. She told me hers while I ate.

She said I reminded her of someone she'd seen a long time ago. I remember dancing for her. I told her I was a bird. A manbird. A hunter. I danced around the kitchen table and sang and pretended to be PowWow Dancer. A bird of dance. A bird of rhythm.

When my mother and grandmother went to town, Ain't Sally took me for a walk around her place. The farm had belonged to her relatives. We went down to the dry gorge and she pointed out all kinds of roots and trees. She asked me if I knew about the plants of the pasture. I said yes. I thought I was lying.

As we walked farther from the house, I remember a hot gusty wind picked up her voice like dust tendrils on bedrock and blew it away from me. I ran to catch the sound. I found Ain't Sally sitting on a granite rock.

—Ala Tek. Indian girl.

—Come and see, on our land, the four winds of the old days will blow through our hair.

Then she tugged at my black braids.

—Come and visit the Snakes, Ala Tek.

—When I was your age they blew across this place like red dust devils on flat neutral plains.

—Can you see them.

—Do you hear the Snake People calling us?

—Yes. I can see them. I hear them. They are naked and wild. Their eyes, like black grapes shining in the Sun, stare back at me.

—They're hungry.

I watch the Snake People eat the fleshy intestines of my uncle's butchered cow. I taste the hot blood, roll it around on my tongue and remember. It makes me sweat.

I watch the Snake People play games around the carcass. And before we walk back into the house, the old woman and me, she runs her crooked fingers across my eyes and says.

—Ala Tek. Indian Girl.

—The ghosts of your ancestors will visit you there.

The rest of the visit blurs. My last memories are from that day. She waves to me from her front porch.

She never explained the Snakes. She only said, "*Che pisa lauchi.* I'll see you. Indians never say good-bye."

I never saw Ain't Sally again until she appeared in my hospital room. I thought she was dead. I didn't know about the Snakes until some twenty-five years later. To make the sign of the snake means:

Comanches are here.

Indians Never Say Good-bye

There she was standing over me. She inched her face close to my face. She put her hands on my face. I remembered her immediately, but did not speak. My eyes blurred. They were hot and heavy. It hurt to look at Ain't Sally. It hurt to see.

I closed my eyes. I felt her cool touch. She chanted. "You will be well. You will not die. *Chim achukma taha che.* You will be well. *Chi pesa taha che.*"

She sang to me. Then I heard her leave.

A woman whose bed was surrounded by white partitions, moaned again. This was not a new sound. It was a constant. Her breath whistled irregularly. There was no escaping the whistle. The whistling sounds were everywhere in the white room. Then they stopped.

Another woman in another bed called out. No answer. She pushed the bell. Women wearing white dresses came into the room. They pushed the partitions back. They said the whistling woman was dead. I went back to sleep. Before the hospital. Before rheumatic fever. Before the dead woman. I had met Ain't Sally. I was seven years old.

Ain't Sally was an ancient Indian relative who lived in Hayrick, outside of Dublin. A place of the Snakes. A place of memory.

Once a base camp for nomadic tribes following buffalo, once a county seat, Hayrick, Texas took its name from a solitary mountain standing in the breadth of open grasslands. Only a state government road sign remains, marking the place of Hayrick. Marking the sign of the Snakes.

The only time we visited Ain't Sally, I rode in the back seat of our green 1950 Chevrolet, and listened to my Indian grandmother tell stories about our family. Chapters went like this:

—Life in a Dugout.

—Making Lye Soap.

—How Grandfather got VD.

I don't remember much of the drive to Hayrick. We drove the rural roads of West Texas. There were two lanes of dust and dirt, stagnant, green-belted river beds and one-lane bridges.

When we arrived at Ain't Sally's the old woman ambled out of a rusted screen door of a paintless wooden house. Breasts sagging, her thin body lacking in strength seemed unable to support her weight. She wore a sleeveless dress that revealed naked brown skin, skin that was no more than a sheath for aging bones. Hairless underarms.

She fed us saltine crackers and cold squirrel dumplings. She asked me questions. She asked me about my secrets. I don't remember having any to tell. She told me hers while I ate.

She said I reminded her of someone she'd seen a long time ago. I remember dancing for her. I told her I was a bird. A manbird. A hunter. I danced around the kitchen table and sang and pretended to be PowWow Dancer. A bird of dance. A bird of rhythm.

When my mother and grandmother went to town, Ain't Sally took me for a walk around her place. The farm had belonged to her relatives. We went down to the dry gorge and she pointed out all kinds of roots and trees. She asked me if I knew about the plants of the pasture. I said yes. I thought I was lying.

As we walked farther from the house, I remember a hot gusty wind picked up her voice like dust tendrils on bedrock and blew it away from me. I ran to catch the sound. I found Ain't Sally sitting on a granite rock.

—Ala Tek. Indian girl.

—Come and see, on our land, the four winds of the old days will blow through our hair.

Then she tugged at my black braids.

—Come and visit the Snakes, Ala Tek.

—When I was your age they blew across this place like red dust devils on flat neutral plains.

CPSIA information can be obtained
at www.ICGtesting.com
Printed in the USA
LVHW012302190622
721628LV00004B/658